D0230998

PHOTOS FIRST

RUTH THOMSON

W

FRANKLIN WATTS

LONDON·SYDNEY

LANCASHIRE COUNTY LIBRARY

30118134173446

Franklin Watts

Published in Great Britain in 2017 by The Watts Publishing Group

Copyright © Franklin Watts 2013

All rights reserved.

Editor: Paul Rockett
Designer: Jason Billin

Dewey no: 770

ISBN: 978 1 4451 1913 7

Printed in Malaysia

MIX
Paper from
responsible sources
FSC
www.fsc.org
FSC® C104740

Franklin Watts
An imprint of
Hachette Children's Group
Part of The Watts Publishing Group
Carmelite House
50 Victoria Embankment
London EC4Y 0DZ

An Hachette UK Company

www.hachette.co.uk

www.franklinwatts.co.uk

Lancashire Library Services	
30118134173446	
PETERS	J779THO
£8.99	31-Mar-2017
NMO	

The author would like to thank the following people for their help with this book:
Virginia Chandler, John Kenward, Brigitte Lardinois, Gilly Lacey, Caroline Pick and
Chloë Thomson.

Picture credits: William Anders/NASA: 22 detail, 23. Ansel Adams Publishing Rights Trust/Corbis: 20 detail,
21. Cecil Beaton/IWM/Getty Images: 44 detail, 45. Jean-Baptiste Sabatier-Blot/wikimedia: 6 detail, 7. Hugo
Burnand. All rights reserved by the British Monarchy: 14 detail, 15. Stephen Dalton/Nature PL: 28 detail, 29.
Robert Doisneau/Gamma-Rapho/Getty Images: 46 detail, 47. Charles C Ebbets/Bettmann/Corbis: 40 detail, 41.
emran/Shutterstock: front cover. Elliott Erwitt/Magnum Photos: 52 detail, 53. Georg Gerster/Panos Pictures: 24
detail, 25. The J. Paul Getty Museum, Los Angeles. © 1986 David Hockney. Pearblossom Highway, 11th-18th
April 1986 #2. Chromogenic print, 181.6 x 271.8 cm, framed 198.1 x 281.9 cm. Andreas Gursky/DACS: 36

Note to parents and teachers

Every effort has been made by the Publishers to ensure that the websites in this book are suitable for children,
that they are of the highest educational value, and that they contain no inappropriate or offensive material.
However, because of the nature of the Internet, it is impossible to guarantee that the contents of these sites
will not be altered. We strongly advise that Internet access is supervised by a responsible adult.

Contents

Introduction

About this book

When photography began, it was an elaborate, expensive, time-consuming, elite activity, using heavy, cumbersome equipment. Today, taking photographs can be instant, cheap and accessible to anyone. Despite the enormous changes in photographic equipment and technology since the 19th century, the purposes of photography have remained essentially the same, whether immortalising, exploring, documenting, revealing or showing us what we can't see with the naked eye.

Divided by themes, this book tells the stories behind some memorable photographs spanning the history of photography, chosen for the vividness or importance of their subject matter, their pioneering photographic technique or their historic significance.

Portrait photography

Before photography was invented, only the very rich could afford to have their likeness painted in a portrait. Early portrait photographers often copied the conventions of painted portraits. Ordinary people dressed in their best clothes and posed in front of painted backdrops with columns and drapes adding a sense of grandeur.

Good portrait photographs reveal something about a person's personality or mood. Close-ups (pp. 11,13) are the most intimate and personal. Wider shots (p. 9) include an environment that suggests a sense of someone's life or work. Group portraits (p. 15), celebrate special or formal occasions where people come together.

Nature photography

Dramatic landscapes and weather, wildlife behaviour and habitats, and the beauty and growth of plants are the main subjects of nature photography. Nature photographers emphasise the marvels of the natural world, often using specialist equipment to freeze motion (pp. 19, 29) or show close-ups (p. 27), or by taking photographs from a long distance (p. 21) or an unusual perspective (p. 25).

Photography as art

People have long claimed that photography is an art discipline in its own right, which people can enjoy for aesthetic pleasure. Today, the works of many contemporary photographers hang alongside paintings in art galleries and museums, and are sold at high prices in auctions, like other fine art. Several fine artists, including Andy Warhol (p. 33) and David Hockney (p. 35), have made one-off artworks using photography.

Documentary photography

Images that provide visual evidence about the reality of particular cultural, political or environmental situations or events are called documentary photographs. Many documentary photographers work on long-term stories about a chosen group of people, including refugees, remote communities, tourists, workers (pp. 41, 55), the rural poor (p. 43) and those in wartime (p .45). Their images are often shocking, attracting public attention and empathy. Other photographers roam cities and shoot otherwise overlooked details of daily life (p. 53). Photojournalists usually work on specific assignments for newspapers and magazines, capturing key visual moments of news events (pp. 49, 57).

Photography as truth?

It has been said that 'the camera never lies', but this is not so. The Cottingley Fairies (p. 39) is a famous example of a hoax photograph and Doisneau's apparently documentary picture (p. 47) was, in fact, staged. All photographs can only be a selected and framed frozen moment, which ignore everything beyond the frame. Photographers have often cropped a photograph for heightened effect (p. 11). Sometimes, they intensify tones or combine two negatives together (p. 31). Today, it is possible to manipulate photographs using powerful computer programs.

Photo thoughts

- 📷 What is the main focus of each photograph in the book?
- 📷 What might have been left out of the image?
- 📷 Which of the photos makes the greatest impression on you? Can you think why?

Louis Daguerre 1844

Jean-Baptiste Sabatier-Blot (French, 1801–1881)

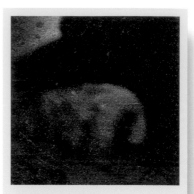

Blow Up

Why do you think Daguerre has his fingers clenched into a fist?

The photograph

This is a portrait of Louis Daguerre, who produced the first permanent photograph. It was named 'daguererotype' after its inventor. In 1839, Daguerre announced his achievement to the French Academy of Sciences. The French government was so impressed that it gave Daguerre a lifetime pension in exchange for the rights to his invention. Daguerreotypes became very popular, especially in America. Sealed with glass to prevent them from tarnishing, the images were framed and kept in velvet-lined leather cases.

Daguerreotypes needed a long exposure and lots of light. Studios had glass roofs to let in as much light as possible. Daguerre would have felt very hot sitting with sunlight shining directly onto his face. His head, neck and back were probably held in braces, so that he could keep perfectly still for the minute-long exposure.

The photographer

To make a daguerreotype, the photographer cleaned and buffed a silver-coated copper plate until it gleamed. He sensitised the plate with chemicals, before putting it in the camera. When he took off the camera lens cap, the plate was exposed to light. After developing the plate over warm mercury vapour, an image appeared. It was fixed (stabilised) with salt water. Each daguerreotype was a unique, fragile, reflective image.

Zoom In ▶

Daguerre wears the clothes of a fashionable man – a dark suit with big buttons, a satin waistcoat, a high collar and a cravat. His pose, with an elbow resting on a table, copies the pose of wealthy people in portrait paintings of his time.

Photo thoughts

- 📷 What impression do you think Daguerre wanted to create with his portrait?
- 📷 Why were images like this considered precious?
- 📷 When photography was invented, artists feared this would be the end of portrait painting. Do you think this has happened?

Jean-Baptiste Sabatier-Blot/wikimedia

"I have seized the light. I have arrested its flight." Louis Daguerre

Pablo Picasso 1949

Gjon Mili (Albanian-American, 1904–1984)

The photograph

Mili was given an assignment by *Life* magazine to visit Picasso, the famous Spanish artist, in the south of France. He showed Picasso his photos of ice skaters leaping in the dark, with minute lights fixed to their skates. These gave Picasso an idea. Using a small electric light in a darkened room, the artist quickly drew the swirling outline of a Minotaur – half bull, half man – in the air. Of course, this fleeting work of art disappeared almost as soon as it was made, but Mili captured it on film for posterity. He was able to capture the entire movement of Picasso's light drawing by using a very slow shutter speed (the time that the shutter remains open).

Blow Up

Picasso drew the Minotaur with a single, unbroken line. How did he draw its eyes?

The photographer

Originally trained as an electrical engineer, Mili was a self-taught photographer. Renowned for his innovations with strobe lighting and long exposures, he specialised in capturing a sequence of actions in a single photo, making time appear frozen. He used this technique to make studies of moving dancers, athletes, musicians and skaters.

Photo thoughts

- 📷 Is this still a Picasso artwork, even if it exists only as a photograph?
- 📷 What words would you use to describe Picasso from looking at this photograph?
- 📷 What movements did Picasso make with his body to create this image?

Zoom In

The plates and dishes on the shelves and the jugs on the floor were all painted by Picasso. He created a huge number of ceramics whilst living in the pottery town of Vallauris between 1948 and 1955.

© Gjon Mili/TimeLifePictures/Getty Images

"To draw, you must close your eyes and sing."

Pablo Picasso

Heroic Guerrilla Fighter 1960

Alberto Díaz Gutiérrez (known as Korda) (Cuban, 1928–2001)

The photograph

Argentinian-born Che Guevara was a charismatic guerrilla commander in the Cuban Revolution and a key member of the new Cuban government. This picture of him was hurriedly snapped at a state funeral for Cuban victims killed in a freighter explosion in Havana's harbour. The image has since become a potent symbol of resistance and radical protest movements. Converted into a simplified, black and white graphic, Che's face has also been hijacked for commercial purposes, reproduced on countless posters, T-shirts, postcards, mugs and in advertisements.

The photographer

Korda was Cuba's top fashion photographer until the Cuban Revolution in 1959. Then he became President Fidel Castro's personal photographer, recording Castro's activities, both in Cuba and abroad. His photographs were often published in the Cuban daily newspaper *Revolucíon*.

Photo thoughts

- Che's shoulders face one direction and his head faces another. What effect does this have?
- How does the contrast of light and dark give Che's face such a powerful presence?
- Why do you think this image has been reproduced so many times?

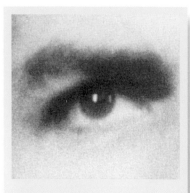

Blow Up

Che's eyes look upwards, past the camera, towards a far horizon. How do you think he was feeling?

Zoom In

Korda's original shot was landscape-shaped, showing Che's head and shoulders against an expanse of sky, with the profile of a man on Che's left and palm leaves on his right. Korda cropped this image very tightly, getting rid of the distracting elements. He reframed the image into a portrait shape, with Che's head filling most of it.

© Korda/Alamy

"This photograph is not the product of knowledge or technique. It was really coincidence, pure luck." Alberto Korda

Afghan Girl 1985

Steve McCurry (American, b.1950)

The photograph

With her piercing green eyes staring straight at us, this portrait of a 12-year-old girl has come to symbolise the upheaval of people during war and the plight of refugees. The photographer, Steve McCurry, shot the image in a refugee camp on the Afghan-Pakistan border. It appeared on the cover of *National Geographic* magazine, accompanying an article about the refugees. No-one knew the name of the girl nor what had happened to her until 2002. After a long search, McCurry and a TV crew discovered her back in her home village in Afghanistan. She was now a married woman with three daughters. Her name is Sharbat Gula.

The photographer

A celebrated photojournalist, McCurry has photographed wars in many countries as well as Afghanistan, including Iraq, Lebanon, Cambodia and the Gulf. On one of his earliest assignments in Afghanistan, he disguised himself in local costume and sewed rolls of film into his clothes to keep them safe.

Photo thoughts

- How does the girl's direct stare make you feel?
- How might the effect of this photograph have differed if the photographer had taken a wider shot?
- If you had to put this photograph into a category, which would you choose: portrait or documentary or both? Why?

Blow Up

What adjectives would you use to descibe the girl's expression?

Zoom In

Notice how the red of the girl's headscarf stands out against the green of the tent in the background and frames her face. Red and green are known as complementary colours. Placed side by side, they make each other seem brighter.

© Steve McCurry/Magnum Photos

"This portrait summed up for me the trauma... of suddenly having to flee your home and end up in a refugee camp, hundreds of miles away." Steve McCurry

Royal Wedding 2011

Hugo Burnand (British, b.1963)

The photograph

The most formal of the three official photographs taken of the Royal Wedding between Prince William and Kate Middleton is this one, showing the two families ranged on either side of the bride and groom. The photographer had less than 30 minutes to take photographs – between the wedding party's return from Westminster Abbey and their appearance on the balcony of Buckingham Palace for the Red Arrow fly past. Burnand had to plan the shoot carefully in advance. He decided where everyone would be positioned and held a dress rehearsal in the Grand Throne Room of the palace, with staff standing in for the families. He placed the two chairs in the exact positions he wanted them to be and lit the room to give the effect of a fine spring morning.

The photographer

Hugo Burnand is an established portrait photographer. He had already taken the official photograph to mark Princes Charles' 60th birthday and the marriage photographs of Prince Charles to the Duchess of Cornwall. He was able to chat and joke with the families, putting everyone at ease, to create relaxed and friendly images.

Photo thoughts

- What does this image tell you about the two families?
- What do the colours and details of the setting contribute to the photograph?
- Compare this wedding photograph with those of your own family. What similarities and differences do you notice?

Blow Up

Do you think that the linked hands of the Duchess of Cornwall and her grand-daughter were posed or spontaneous?

Zoom In

Notice how the newly-wed couple stand out from their families, framed by the dark velvet canopy behind them. William and Kate's arms are linked and lifted up to emphasise their togetherness.

"From where I was, and from their point of view, it was two families coming together..." *Hugo Burnand*

Hugo Burnand. All rights reserved by the British Monarchy.

Meily Mendoza Singing to her Doll 2011

Cristina Garcia Rodero (Spanish, b. 1949)

The photograph

This intimate photograph of Meily Mendoza is one of the portraits that Rodero shot for a photo essay of Baracoa, an isolated city surrounded by mountains on the far eastern coast of Cuba. Her photographs commemorate the 500th anniversary of Baracoa, Cuba's oldest settlement, founded by Spanish colonisers in 1511. Meily seems totally unaware of the camera, singing lovingly to the doll she holds tightly in her arms. Strangely, the doll seems to look out at the viewer instead.

Rodero spent several weeks in the city, documenting scenes of daily life in streets, shops, schools, homes and fields, as well as taking a series of striking portraits of some of Baracoa's inhabitants.

The photographer

Rodero studied painting before she took up photography. She has specialised in documenting traditions, rituals and festivities, both religious and pagan, first in Spain, then in other parts of Europe and more recently in Haiti. She spends considerable time with the people that she is going to photograph, so that, in her own words, 'being with them makes me invisible'.

Photo thoughts

- Do you think Meily Mendoza posed for this photograph?
- Does it feel as if the photographer was 'invisible' to Meily?
- What can you tell about the people of Baracoa from this portrait of Meily?

Blow Up

How does this photograph capture Meily's affection for her doll?

Zoom In

This photograph is rich with textures and pattern. Meily stands in front of a roughly plastered wall. Her dress is decorated with lace and embossed with embroidery. Her doll wears a hat, tunic and shoes in matching flowery patterned fabric.

© Cristina Garcia Rodero/Magnum Photos

"I'm interested in people who are never going to make the news." Cristina Garcia Rodero

Galloping Horses 1878

Eadweard Muybridge (British, 1830–1904)

The photograph

Hoping to breed faster racehorses, Leland Stanford, a wealthy American racehorse owner, wanted to know whether a horse lifted all four hooves off the ground when it galloped. No-one could see this with the naked eye. He hired Eadweard Muybridge, an Anglo-American photographer, to discover the answer. Muybridge set up 12 plate glass cameras in a line along a racetrack on Stanford's stud farm. The high-speed shutter on each camera was triggered by the horse's movement over trip wires.

The photographer

Muybridge had been a well-known landscape photographer in California. After taking this horse sequence, he spent several years taking thousands more pictures of animals and people in motion, and compiled them into a book. Modern animators still use his book as reference today. Muybridge toured the country showing his slides on a zoopraxiscope, a projection device he invented.

Photo thoughts

- Which of the photographs prove that all the horse's hooves lift off the ground?
- Are the frames in the sequence all different or are any identical?
- Muybridge later used 24 cameras instead of 12. Why might that be better?

Blow Up

Does the position of the rider change much in the sequence?

Zoom In

Follow each of the horse's four legs in turn, to work out how the front and back legs bend and stretch in relationship to one another. Notice when only the front or the back legs are on the ground.

© Eadweard Muybridge/Corbis

"The painter constructs. The photographer discloses."

Susan Sontag (writer of *On Photography*)

The Tetons and the Snake River 1942

Ansel Adams (American, 1902–1984)

The photograph

Rocky mountains, rippling water, tree-covered land and cloud-filled sky – in Adams' carefully-framed image, all these elements of nature are in balance. They create a feeling of beauty, peace and timelessness, untouched by human presence. By showing the river snaking from one side of the photograph to the other, Adams leads our eye through the landscape to the mountains faraway, just as if we were there.

Adams photographed with a bulky, large-format camera. Using the smallest aperture and a slow shutter speed, he was able to make sure that the distant mountains were in just as sharp focus and detail as the foreground trees.

The photographer

Adams was a masterful photographer, who shared his passion and knowledge about photography through writings, lectures and hands-on workshops. He was also a campaigning environmentalist, who used his photographs of the wilderness to persuade the US government to preserve areas of natural beauty as national parks.

Photo thoughts

- Which parts of this picture are whitest and blackest? How many in-between shades of grey can you identify?
- What effect does the high angle of this image have on the way that you see it?
- Why do you think this picture was chosen as one of the 115 images sent aboard the *Voyager* spacecraft into outer space?

Blow Up

How does the sky help give the scene a sense of grandeur?

Zoom In

By carefully controlling both the exposure and the development of the film, Adams was able to create a dramatic atmosphere. He ensured that the paler watery parts – river and snow – contrast very strongly with the dark foreground trees and the rocks.

© Ansel Adams Publishing Rights Trust/Corbis

"A good photograph is knowing where to stand." Ansel Adams

Earthrise 1968

William Anders (American, b. 1933)

The photograph

Hailed as the most influential environmental photograph ever taken, this shot shows a view of the Earth rising above the Moon's surface, but otherwise alone in space. It was taken through the tiny window of a lunar module by William Anders, one of the three-man crew on the *Apollo 8* mission, the first manned voyage to orbit the Moon. The astronauts' job was to take images of the Moon's surface, including the far side (which can never be seen from Earth), scouting out possible landing spots for future missions. But perhaps this photograph has done a far more important job, reminding people of the fragility and finite resources of our own planet.

The photographer

As flight engineer on the mission, Anders' job was to test all the systems for simulating a lunar landing. Frank Borman, the mission commander, took most of the photographs of the Moon. It was only by chance that Anders glanced out of the window, spotted the Earth appearing and quickly snapped this awesome photograph.

Photo thoughts

📷 Why do you think this picture gave rise to the idea of 'Spaceship Earth'?

📷 How does this picture of the Earth make you feel?

📷 What caption would you give to this photograph?

Blow Up

The Earth appears to be lying on its side from this view. Can you spot the west coast of Africa and the snow of Antarctica?

Zoom In ▶

The desolate, dead grey surface of the Moon is pitted with craters, where comets and meteorites bombarded it in the long distant past. There could hardly be a stronger contrast in colour with the brilliant blues and swirling whites of the Earth.

William Anders/NASA

"We came all this way to explore the Moon and the most important thing is that we discovered the Earth." William Anders

Camel Caravan 1976

Georg Gerster (Swiss, b. 1928)

Blow Up

What time of day do you think it was when Gerster took this photograph?

The photograph

Given special personal permission by the Empress of Iran, Gerster took hundreds of aerial pictures of Iran, including this one of a camel caravan making its way along a sandy road. From this high, unusual viewpoint, it is hard to identify the camels. However, the long shadows cast by their bodies make them instantly easy to recognise, despite their elongated, spindly legs. Their loads and riders are also revealed in silhouette. From this perspective, the human intervention of the road appears as a slash across the desert landscape.

The photographer

Gerster has spent 50 years taking aerial photographs of towns and cities, mountains, deserts, coasts and archaeological sites in more than 100 countries. His pictures have revealed long-lost structures of ancient cultures, natural shifts in the landscape, the shapes of growing cities and changes in land cultivation.

Photo thoughts

- What problems do you think Gerster might encounter doing aerial photography?
- How does Gerster suggest the enormity of the desert?
- Why do you think Gerster took this particular picture?

Zoom In ▶

Gerster composed the image so that the road cuts diagonally straight across its centre, cropping the camel caravan both front and back. This helps give a feeling of movement, as well as the sense of a long road.

© Georg Gerster/Panos Pictures

"Altitude provides overview, overview provides insight, while insight eventually, I hope, leads to respect." Georg Gerster

Sunflower No. 4 1991

Thomas Struth (German, b.1954)

The photograph

Struth was asked to take photographs to decorate patients' rooms in a new hospital in Winterthur, Switzerland. For each of the 37 rooms, he photographed a different local landscape, with a path leading through vineyards, forests, farmland or gardens to a distant horizon. Struth also shot close-ups of familiar flowers with vibrant colours, such as this sunflower, roses, tulips and dandelions, as well as buds and twigs.

A large-scale, landscape print was hung on the wall opposite each bed, for the patient to enjoy. Two of the plant images, enlarged to poster size, were hung side by side behind each bed, cheering up visitors coming to see their ill relative or friend.

The photographer

Struth is one of Germany's most famous art photographers. His large-scale works include family portraits, images of museum visitors looking at famous works of art and shots of complex, contemporary technology and global development.

Photo thoughts

- 📷 Why do you think Struth chose to photograph views and plants of the local environment?
- 📷 Why might Struth have chosen to highlight single flowers, like this one?
- 📷 How might flower pictures in sick rooms influence patients' and visitors' experience of the hospital?

Blow Up

What difference do you notice between the foreground flower and the background?

Zoom In ▶

The sunflower head was shot very close-up, creating an intimate and powerful flower portrait. Every detail of its multi-coloured, pointy petals and swirly seed head is crisp, clear and bright.

© Thomas Struth

"(When) I am taking a photograph, I am conscious that I am constructing images, rather than taking snapshots." Thomas Struth

Ladybird Take-off 2007

Stephen Dalton (British, b.1937)

The photograph

It convincingly appears that this photograph was taken in nature. In fact, Stephen Dalton built a 'biologically truthful' arrangement on a tabletop. Here, he could direct insects to a specific spot and photograph them in mid-flight.

Since suitable equipment did not already exist for capturing movement at the right moment, Dalton spent two years creating his own photographic set-up – developing his own high-speed flash units, light sensors, transformers and home-made shutters.

The photographer

A pioneer in nature photography, Stephen Dalton was the first to capture pin-sharp images of insects in flight, with their fluttering wings frozen. He has shot other unusual photographs of animals in mid-motion, such as leaping frogs, swooping birds and ghostly owls, in controlled outdoor set-ups.

Photo thoughts

- 📷 What details of this ladybird might not be visible to the naked eye?
- 📷 How does having the plant stem help the composition of the photograph?
- 📷 How does this picture make you feel about nature?

Blow Up

Where do you think the light is coming from in this photograph? How can you tell?

Zoom In ▶

The ladybird looks as if it is about to land on a plant, but actually, it is taking off backwards! Dalton was only able to make this sort of discovery using his high-speed photographic system.

© Stephen Dalton/Narure PL

"The thrill of seeing for the first time how these little creatures moved their wings and manoeuvre through the air ... was overwhelming." Stephen Dalton

Io + Gatto (I + Cat) 1932

Wanda Wulz (Italian, 1903–1984)

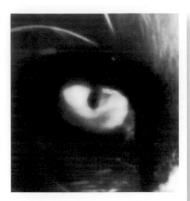

The photograph

The striking self-portrait of Wanda Wulz, an experimental Italian photographer, was created by a technique called sandwich negatives. She took two separate pictures, one of herself and one of Pippo, her cat. In the darkroom, she put the two negatives one on top of the other and printed a single, merged image. In areas, such as Wanda's neck and the right-hand side of her face, where the negative was thin (in deep shadow), details from the cat negative stand out most strongly. In areas, such as Wanda's light fur collar and the pale left-hand side of her face, where the negative was denser (bright), details of the cat scarcely come through.

The photographer

The third generation of a family of portrait photographers in Trieste, Italy, Wanda Wulz was taught by her father and ran her own portrait studio from 1928. She briefly joined the Futurist movement and showed some of her experimental prints at their photographic exhibition.

Photo thoughts

- 📷 What elements of the photograph are of Wanda?
- 📷 What was the most important detail to line up in both photographs?
- 📷 Which, in your opinion, stands out more – the cat or Wanda, or are they both equal?

Blow Up

Can you distinguish the cat's eye from the photographer's eye?

Zoom In ▶

Some parts of the cat, such as its long whiskers, furry bib, wet nose and white paw are clearly identifiable. Notice too the ghostly shapes of its pointed ears, which stick out on either side of Wanda's head.

© Wanda Wulz /Topfoto

"If man could be crossed with the cat it would improve man, but it would deteriorate the cat." Mark Twain (writer)

Marilyn Diptych 1962

Andy Warhol (American, 1928–1987)

The photograph

Marilyn Monroe was the most famous film star of her time. Photographs of her appeared endlessly in magazines, newspapers and publicity stills. After her death in 1962, Andy Warhol bought a publicity photograph of Marilyn, which he cropped, enlarged and transferred onto a silkscreen (a kind of stencil). He pressed black paint through the silkscreen, creating a painted image identical to the original photograph. He duplicated the image 50 times, varying the amount of black paint, to make either distinct, precise images or blurred, faded ones. He painted half the faces in vivid, unreal colours, suggesting Marilyn's glamorous, but artificial, image in life. These contrast sharply with the black and white faces, reminding viewers of her sad suicide.

The photographer

Andy Warhol was obsessed by both fame and death. He made photographic silkscreen portraits of other famous people of the 1960s, including the singer Elvis Presley, Jackie Kennedy, widow of President Kennedy, and Mao Tse-Tung, the leader of China.

Photo thoughts

- Why do you think Warhol duplicated Marilyn's image so many times?
- Why do you think the black and white portraits become increasingly faded?
- Are these images still photographs?

Blow Up

Why do you think Warhol portrayed Marilyn so heavily made-up with strong red lipstick and blue eyeshadow?

Zoom In

Warhol's mechanical way of repeating images questioned the role of the artist in creating art. It also challenged the idea that a portrait was only unique and authentic if it was hand-painted.

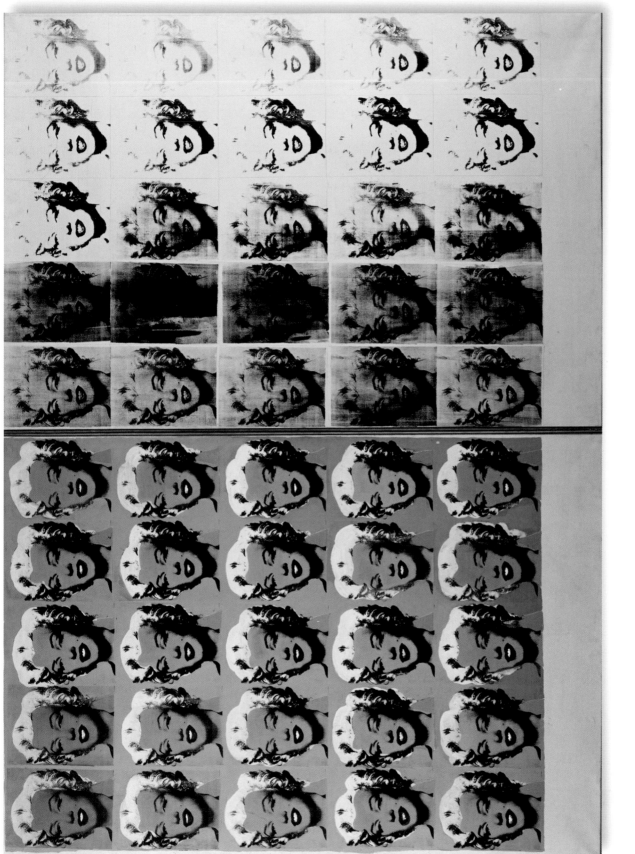

© The Warhol Foundation/Superstock

"In the future, everyone will be world-famous for fifteen minutes."

Andy Warhol

Pearblossom Highway 1986

David Hockney (British, b.1937)

The photograph

Measuring almost 2m high by 3m wide, this huge image of a Californian highway is a photographic collage that David Hockney called a 'joiner'. He built it up from hundreds of overlapping photos, taken from different viewpoints over eight days. Hockney shot everything close up, to pull viewers into the picture. He took the road signs from up a ladder and crouched at ground level to take the rubbish on the roadside. He walked down the highway to take the trees and the horizon. The final picture, with its multiple viewpoints and sharp details, shows a far more panoramic view than any wide-angle photograph could ever show. It is not, however, true to life. Hockney moved the signs closer together and chose where to position the large tree.

The photographer

Originally best known for his paintings, printmaking and stage designs, David Hockney has made pictures with all sorts of technology, experimenting with photography, faxes, colour copies, laser prints and, most recently, with split screen videos and the iPad.

Photo thoughts

- Can you see places in this image where Hockney has looked down on the road?
- How can you tell that Hockney photographed the road signs close up?
- What seems odd about the Pearblossom Highway sign?

Blow Up

How would a single photograph of a tree differ from this one made up of multiple shots?

Zoom In

The image depicts the viewpoint of both driver and passenger. The right-hand side highlights signs drivers have to follow. The left-hand side includes small details, such as the roadside litter, that passengers, with leisure to look around, might notice.

"The picture is about driving without the car being in it." David Hockney

The J. Paul Getty Museum, Los Angeles. © 1986 David Hockney

Photos First **35**

99 Cent 1999

Andreas Gursky (German, b.1955)

The photograph

Shot with a large-format, wide-angle camera, Gursky's huge photographic print (2 x 3m) shows a downtown Los Angeles discount store. The apparently endless rows of tidy shelves are shot from a high viewpoint that shoppers would never have themselves. Gursky digitally manipulated the image to create an epic, perfect scene, overflowing with abundance and brightness. It gives us a strong sense of how the browsing shoppers might feel, confronted by such an overwhelming and excessive choice of mass-produced, colourfully-packaged goods.

The photographer

Gursky is inspired by our contemporary, globalised world of large workspaces, shops, hotels, flats and crowd-filled events. He makes the most of digital technology, piecing together multiple shots of an image to create detailed, panoramic and, often, grid-like compositions. He also intensifies colour and contrast. His prints are so enormous that they need to be viewed from a distance to see the whole composition, as well as close-up to appreciate the sharply-focused details.

Photo thoughts

- What do you think Gursky wanted us to think about when we view this image?
- What elements in this picture give it a sense of order and stillness? What breaks the order?
- What effect does Gursky achieve by making the colours so vivid?

Blow Up

What do you notice about the ceiling?

Zoom In

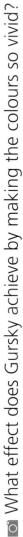

Gursky has manipulated the image so that the horizontal shelves and upright columns form a grid with the goods in groups of repeating colours. Hold the book at arm's length and squint at the image. It will look almost as if it is an abstract pattern.

"I stand at a distance, like a person from another world."

Andreas Gursky

© Andreas Gursky / VG Bild-Kunst / DACS 2013

Cottingley Fairies 1917

Elsie Wright (British, 1901–1988)

The photograph

In 1917, Frances Griffiths and Elsie Wright, young cousins living in Cottingley in Yorkshire, claimed they played with fairies in nearby woods. To prove it, Elsie borrowed a camera from her father. To his surprise, when he developed the photograph, this portrait of Frances with dancing fairies was revealed. In 1920, it came to the attention of Sir Arthur Conan Doyle, creator of the Sherlock Holmes books and a believer in spiritualism. He not only believed the photograph was genuine, but used it and others to illustrate articles and a book claiming that fairies existed. It was only in 1983 that Elsie admitted that their fairy photographs were, in fact, hoaxes! She had drawn and painted the fairies on cardboard, cut them out, stuck them in place with hatpins and then photographed them.

The photographer

Elsie Wright was 16 when she took this photograph. She had some art training and probably copied the fairies from drawings in a book. The fairy photographs dogged her life and, as she later admitted, she was far too embarrassed to confess the truth about them, after they had managed to fool such a prominent person as Conan Doyle.

Photo thoughts

- What do you think might have helped convince people that the fairies were real?
- What might make you think this photo was a hoax?
- How does the setting help add to the atmosphere of the photograph?

Blow Up

What difference do you notice between the lighting on Frances and on the fairies?

Zoom In

Those who believed that the fairies were fake used the argument that their hairstyles seemed very modern – not something real fairies might be expected to concern themselves with!

© Elsie Wright/Topfoto

"It was just Elsie and I having a bit of fun…" Frances Griffiths

Lunchtime atop a Skyscraper 1932

Charles C. Ebbets (American, 1905 – 1978)

Blow Up

How did Ebbets dramatise the height of the beam on which the men are sitting?

Zoom In

It seems incredible that the workers can seem so relaxed, lunching 260m (800ft) up in the air. They chat, smile, eat and hold lunchboxes. One is lighting another's cigarette. Another has an empty whisky bottle in his hand.

The photograph

Skyscraper building boomed in New York in the 1930s. Contractors took advantage of workers during the Great Depression, when unemployment reached 25 per cent. Desperate men took perilous, lowly-paid construction jobs to support their families. Ebbet's breathtaking photograph celebrates these tough men, taking their lunch break on a crossbeam on the unfinished 69th floor of the GE Building, part of the Rockefeller Center. The ends of the beam are out of sight, so the men appear to float in the sky, high above any of the other tall buildings. Central Park stretches out on the right-hand side behind them.

The photographer

Ebbets was a fearless photographer, who even risked taking aerial shots lying on the tail of a plane. He was also a daring hunter, pilot, wrestler and racing car driver, and explored unmapped areas of the Florida Everglades, photographing rare wildlife and the life of the Native American Seminole tribe.

Photo thoughts

- Where do you think the photographer was positioned to take this shot?
- What clues tell you that this was a staged publicity shot to promote this new skyscraper?
- Why is this photograph considered 'an icon of American optimism and ingenuity'?

© Charles C Ebbets/Bettmann/Corbis

"Architecture is the will of an epoch translated into space."

Ludwig Mies van der Rohe (architect)

Migrant Mother 1936

Dorothea Lange (American, 1895–1965)

The photograph

The Great Depression in America was followed in the 1930s by droughts that turned prairie farmland to parched dust. Thousands of poverty-struck families migrated to California hoping to find work, ending up in squalid campsites.

Lange's potent photograph of a hungry, destitute mother with her unkempt children pressed up against her at a pea-pickers' camp has become an enduring image of the Depression. Published in the *San Francisco News*, the photograph spurred the federal government to send 20,000 pounds of food to Californian migrant workers.

The photographer

Dorothea Lange was one of a team of 11 photographers employed in 1935, by the Farm Security Administration, to document the lives of migrant workers. Their photographs were used to publicise the devastating hardship of rural people.

Photo thoughts

- Lange asked the two older children to turn their heads for this photograph. Why might she have done this?
- Lange shot five pictures, starting at a distance, showing details of the family's makeshift tent and muddy fields, then coming closer. Why do you think the public found this close-up so shocking?
- What details in this picture show the family's poverty?

Blow Up

What adjectives would you use to describe the mother's expression?

Zoom In ▶

The tightly-framed portrait focuses on the family, with the mother at the centre. Usually in portraits, people look towards the camera, but here the mother gazes into the distance, her two children look away and the baby is fast asleep.

© Dorothea Lange/Corbis

"The camera is an instrument that teaches people how to see without a camera." Dorothea Lange

Air-raid Victim, London Blitz 1940

Cecil Beaton (British, 1904–1980)

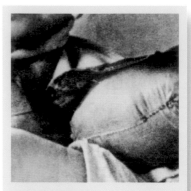

The photograph

During the Second World War, between September 1940 and May 1941, the German Luftwaffe (airforce) repeatedly bombed big cities in the UK, in strikes known as the Blitz. Millions of houses were destroyed and more than 200,000 civilians were killed or injured.

Three-year-old Eileen Dunne, one of the injured, was photographed in her hospital bed by Cecil Beaton. Featured on the cover of the American magazine *Life*, simply captioned 'Air-raid victim', this poignant image of a suffering innocent summed up the random violence of war. It brought home to Americans the reality of the Blitz and the need to help Britain in its fight against Nazism.

The photographer

Best known for his stylish, elegant photographs of the rich and famous, Beaton was also a talented writer, painter and illustrator. Commissioned by the Ministry of Information to document the war, Beaton took more than 7,000 photographs in China, Burma and India, as well as in Britain.

Photo thoughts

📷 How far away did Beaton stand to take this photograph?

📷 How do you think Beaton wanted people to feel when they saw this picture?

📷 Do you think this is a more, or less, convincing image about the nature of war than one of injured soldiers?

Blow Up

How does the inclusion of Eileen's well-worn toy add to the atmosphere of the image?

Zoom In ▶

Beaton deliberately framed this shot to tug at people's heart-strings. Centrally-positioned, framed by the bars of her bed, propped up by a big pillow, Eileen seems alone and vulnerable. She stares straight at the viewer, demanding our attention.

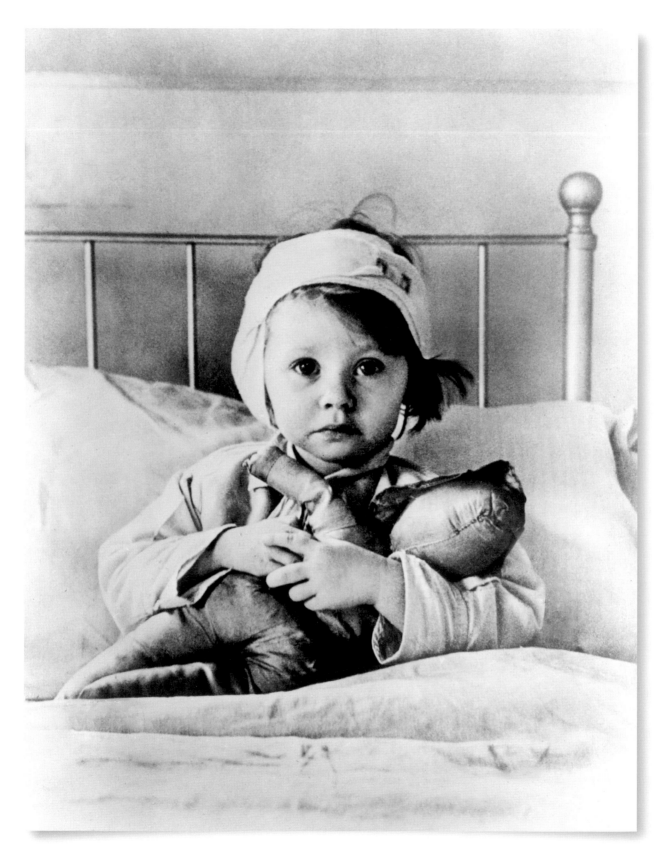

© Cecil Beaton/IWM/Getty Images

"Goering's attacks on London achieve little but the maiming and slaughtering of children."

Illustrated London News picture caption, September 21, 1940

The Kiss by the Hotel de Ville 1950

Robert Doisneau (French, 1912–1994)

The photograph

Considered one of the most romantic and popular photos ever taken, it has been reproduced on more than 500,000 posters and 400,000 postcards. The picture was taken for a photo spread about Paris lovers for *Life* magazine. The couple in the photo were believed to be two anonymous lovers caught unaware. Their identities remained a mystery until 1992, when a couple claiming to be the two in the shot, took Doisneau to court for having taken their picture without their knowledge. This forced Doisneau to reveal that the shot had actually been staged. He had witnessed the couple kiss in the street and had asked them to repeat it for his photograph.

The photographer

French photographer Robert Doisneau is largely known for his street photography. He captured playful, amusing images of different social classes in the streets of his hometown, Paris. He worked briefly as a fashion photographer for *Vogue*, but didn't enjoy photographing beautiful women in elegant surroundings and left to continue photographing street culture.

Photo thoughts

- No one in the photo is looking at the couple. What does this add to the experience?
- What gives the image a sense of motion, as if it were caught quickly?
- Does the photo appear less romantic once you know that it was staged?

Blow Up

How does this passing woman make the photo feel more real?

Zoom In

The only people in focus are the kissing couple and the woman just behind them. The apparently messy composition, with figures cropped on both sides, makes the photo appear as if the kiss was caught, rather than posed.

© Robert Doisneau/Gamma-Rapho/Getty Images

"I don't photograph life as it is, but life as I would like it to be."

Robert Doisneau

Muhammad Ali versus Sonny Liston 1965

Neil Leifer (American, b.1942)

The photograph

The American magazine, *Sports Illustrated*, sent two photographers to cover the second world heavyweight boxing fight between Sonny Liston and Muhammad Ali (then known as Cassius Clay). Within a few minutes of the first round, Liston fell to the ground and lay prone, seemingly unable to get up. Leifer captured the dramatic instant when Ali stood over Liston, shouting, 'Get up and fight, sucker!' The shot sums up the essence of Ali's force, confidence and swagger. Eventually, Liston stood up and Ali knocked him out.

The photographer

Fanatical about sport, Leifer has taken photographs of many major sporting events, including football and baseball matches, motor races, golf tournaments, as well as winter and summer Olympics. Boxing is his favourite sport and he covered 60 of Muhammad Ali's fights.

Photo thoughts

📷 What is your impression of Muhammad Ali's character?

📷 How does the lighting contribute to the drama of the scene?

📷 Leifer said, 'What separates a great sports photographer from an ordinary one is that when they get lucky, they don't miss.' What was lucky for Leifer with this shot?

Blow Up

What view would Herb Scharfman, the other *Sports Illustrated* photographer, have seen?

Zoom In

Compare the bodies and gestures of the two boxers. Ali's arm and leg muscles are taut and prominent. His right arm is poised to lash out. Liston's body is floppy. Both arms are raised above his head, as if in a position of surrender.

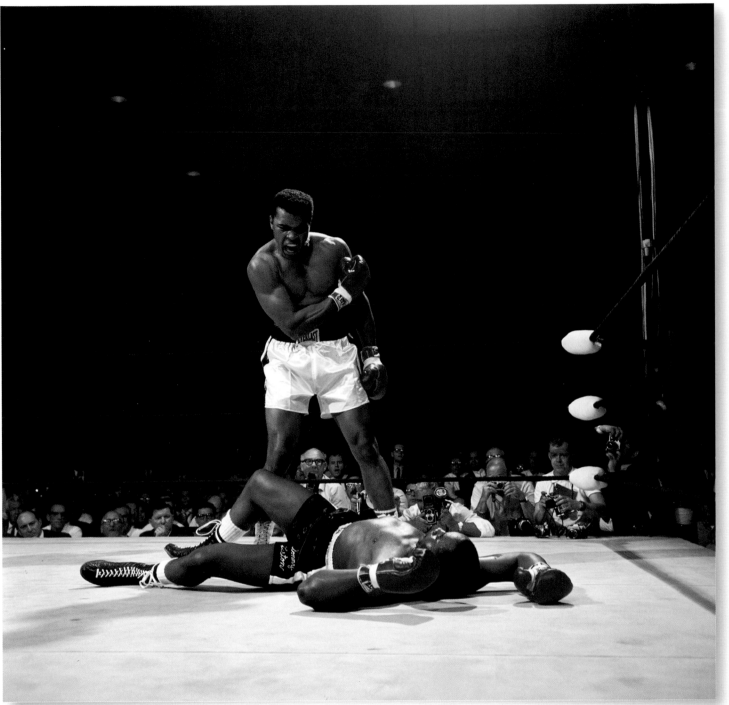

© Neil Leifer/Sports Illustrated/Getty Images

"When you're shooting ringside, you feel what the fighters feel." Neil Leifer

Buzz Aldrin on the Moon 1969

Neil Armstrong (American, 1930–2012)

The photograph

Neil Armstrong took the majority of photos from the *Apollo 11* mission, and so there are not many images of him. However, you can see him reflected in Buzz Aldrin's gold-plated visor, making this picture a double portrait.

An estimated 500 million people watched the Moon landing and Aldrin sees this image as bringing the world together, with the reflection showing it to be a shared experience. However, there are many people who believe that the photos taken were all fakes and that they had been set up in a film studio. They question the high quality of the image and the fact that there are no stars in the sky.

The photographer

Known more for being the first man on the Moon than for taking photos, Neil Armstrong was the main photographer of *Apollo 11*'s mission to the Moon. He has received praise for the composition of his images, especially since he had no photographic training.

Photo thoughts

- Is this still a portrait of Buzz Aldrin, even though you cannot see his face?
- How does having the reflection of Neil Armstrong change the feeling of the photo?
- What might make you think this photo was staged?

Blow Up

Aside from the photographer and the spacecraft, what else can you see in the reflection?

Zoom In

There is an astronaut against the horizon of the Moon. There are footprints in the foreground and a piece of equipment at the bottom right. You can see this in the reflection in the visor, along with the spacecraft and the photographer.

Neil Armstrong/ NASA

"In this one moment, the world came together in peace for all mankind." Buzz Aldrin

New York City 1974

Elliott Erwitt (American, b.1928)

The photograph

Does this photograph make you smile? This minute, forlorn Chihuahua would make an amusing image on its own, with its enormous ears and little legs, wearing a knitted coat and a ridiculous, oversized hat firmly knotted under its chin. What makes it much funnier is its juxtaposition with the shiny knee-high boots of its owner who towers way above it, and the front paws of a huge Great Dane, standing in an almost identical pose beside her. Shooting from the tiny dog's eyeline, so that the rest of the owner and the back legs of the Great Dane are left out of the image, Erwitt created a comical shot that makes you look twice.

The photographer

Elliott Erwitt believes that you can find pictures anywhere. He has a keen eye for spotting comic and absurd moments in everyday life, and capturing them with impeccable timing. He is skilled at composing his shots in the camera, rarely cropping or manipulating images afterwards. He has frequently photographed dogs.

Photo thoughts

- How would this picture be different if it had been taken from further away?
- Who is this picture about – the dogs or their owner? Why do you think this?
- What do you think of the title for this picture? What would you have titled it?

Blow Up

Where do you think the photographer positioned himself to take this view of the dog?

Zoom In

The composition is very precise. Notice the rhythm of the vertical lines of legs, which fill the central portion of the image in sharp focus. These stand out boldly against the light, fuzzy background.

"To me, photography is the art of observing. It's about finding something interesting in an ordinary place." Elliott Erwitt

© Elliott Erwitt/Magnum Photos

Serra Pelada Gold Mine 1986

Sebastião Salgado (Brazilian, b.1944)

The photograph

An outstanding photojournalist, Salgado spent three weeks documenting this mine in a remote part of Brazil, his home country. Gold had been discovered here some years earlier, attracting 50,000 hopeful prospectors. Some of his photographs, like this long shot, show the enormity of the man-made mine, with carved-out hollows and terraces, and long, rickety ladders leaning against its steep sides. The packed crowd of miners, shifting their loads of earth, appear to move as one, in a continuous flow, like ants. By contrast, Salgado's close-ups focus on the strength and determination of individual miners, covered in mud, who clamber up slopes and ladders, every sinew straining.

The photographer

Salgado travels the world, for several years at a time, to take photographs on chosen themes. After photographing the gold miners, he went on to shoot other examples of hard physical labour in 26 countries – including ship-building in Poland, sulphur-mining in Indonesia, sugar-cane cutting in Cuba and digging the Eurotunnel in England.

Photo thoughts

- 📷 How does the absence of sky affect the atmosphere of this image?
- 📷 Why do you think Salgado prefers to shoot in black and white, rather than colour?
- 📷 Why do you think Salgado called this view 'a vision from the Middle Ages'? What is most obviously missing from it?

Blow Up

Does the mining look organised or chaotic? What makes you say that?

Zoom In

Taken from a distance, this vertical image emphasises the depth of the mine. Salgado's composition, with workers cropped off on all four sides, suggests that the mine stretches on and on, well beyond this frame.

© Sebastião Selgado/Amazonas Images/*nbpictures

"I'm a journalist. My life's on the road, my studio is the planet." Sebastião Selgado

Blow Up

What do the arrows and lines on the road add to the power of the image?

Zoom In

The tight view of a very wide road and the tanks shot on a diagonal help give this image much power. The lone man seems so vulnerable against these four huge machines, yet he has managed to stop them.

Tank Man 1989

Jeff Widener (American, b.1956)

The photograph

In June 1989, hundreds of thousands of students occupied Tiananmen Square in Beijing, China to protest against government corruption, and to demand freedom of speech and freedom of the press. The government ordered the People's Liberation Army to clear the square. They opened fire on the unarmed protesters and there were many casualties.

Still banned in China, more than 20 years after it was taken, this photograph of a lone man blocking a line of tanks on its way to Tiananmen Square, has become an iconic image of this incident.

The photographer

An experienced press photographer, Widener risked arrest to take this picture from a 6th floor hotel balcony after the army had taken control. Quick thinking, he enlisted the help of a passing American student, who not only accompanied him as a 'hotel guest' past security police into the hotel room, but also delivered Widener's film to the Associated Press office, hidden in his underwear.

Photo thoughts

 The man is standing on a road crossing, holding two shopping bags.
How do these details affect your view of the image?

What does the inclusion of the street light add to the atmosphere of the photo?

Why do you think this picture has become so iconic?

© Jeff Widener/AP/PAI

"The faceless man represents all of us in the fight for democracy."

Jeff Widener

Barcelona 2011

Martin Parr (British, b.1952)

The photograph

Tourists throng to the Park Güell in Barcelona, to see its quirky buildings and benches with intricate mosaics designed by the Catalan architect, Antoni Gaudi. But, as Martin Parr's photograph so wittily shows, contemporary tourists spend their time taking photographs, rather than enjoying the experience of meandering through this peaceful pleasure garden.

Parr has taken photographs at many famous tourist sites around the world. However, he is far more interested in capturing the way tourists behave and the guides, vendors and signs around these sites, than in the sites themselves.

The photographer

Parr is a documentary chronicler of contemporary everyday life, often with a humorous or ironic eye. He has become interested in the effects of globalisation, consumerism and excessive wealth, and tourism. He is an avid collector of postcards, photography books, badges and political ephemera, which he sometimes exhibits alongside his photos.

Photo thoughts

- Parr believes that 'we photograph ourselves at tourist sites to be reassured that we are part of the recognisable world'. Do you agree with this view?
- When people used film, which was costly to buy and process, they took fewer photographs. What are the advantages and disadvantages of being able to take endless digital photographs?
- Do you think that taking photographs is the best way of keeping an experience?

Blow Up

Is anyone in Parr's photograph looking at the site without holding a camera?

Zoom In

This image supports Parr's claim that photography is the greatest democratic art form of our time. People of all ages have arranged themselves so they all get a good view, without other tourists in the way. Notice how some of them stand on a ledge.

© Martin Parr/Magnum Photos

"Now it is impossible for me to shoot a photograph where someone is NOT taking a picture or posing for one." Martin Parr

Glossary

aerial photographs photographs taken from an aeroplane, helicopter or hot-air balloon of land or sea below

background the part of a photo that appears furthest away from the viewer

close-up a shot where the camera takes a detail rather than the whole of a subject

commission where a person or an organisation asks a photographer to take photographs in return for paying a fee

composition how all the elements of a photograph fit together

contrast the degree of difference between the darkest and lightest parts of a photograph

cropped where an image has been cut off at one or more edges, often done to improve the composition of a photograph

depth of field the distance in a photograph from the closest point in focus to the most distant point still in focus

developing a chemical process making an exposed photographic image visible

digital camera a camera that stores image data in digital format, which can be downloaded onto a computer and, if desired, manipulated

engraving a print made from a photograph that has been transferred onto a metal plate

exposure the amount of light that is allowed to reach photographic film or an image sensor

flash unit an instrument which creates a bright, brief, artificial burst of light to illuminate a dark scene, when a photograph is being taken

foreground the part of a photograph that appears closest to the viewer

frame the border that encloses a photograph

Futurism an artistic movement that started in Italy in about 1910. Its artists were inspired by, and tried to express, the dynamism of contemporary life and the speed and force of modern machinery

grid a network of vertical and horizontal lines spaced uniformly

horizon the line where the land (or sea) meets the sky

juxtaposition the placement of two or more things side by side

large-format camera a camera that uses film that is 4 x 5in (10 x 13cm) or larger, often used for landscape photography

negative photographic film that has been exposed to light – where the light parts appear dark and the dark parts appear light. A negative is used for making a photographic print

panorama a wide view in all directions, often of a large area of land or a city

photojournalist someone who tells a news story through photographs, often with added text

point of view the angle from which a viewer or photographer sees a person, object or scene

portrait an image of a particular person or group of people

pose the deliberate positioning of head, body, arms and legs by someone in front of a camera

shutter the part of a camera that opens and closes to let light through for a certain length of time

silhouette an outline filled with shadow, showing the shape of a person or thing against a light background

strobe a lamp that produces very short and intense light flashes

tone in a photograph, the quality of light or darkness

viewfinder the part of a camera that a photographer looks through to frame and focus a picture

viewpoint the position, angle and direction from which a photographer takes a picture

wide-angle lens a lens with a wider angle view than a standard lens

zoopraxiscope a device that projects discs of still images in rapid succession, giving an impression of movement

Find out more

Ansel Adams

Iconic landscape photographs

- *Moonrise, Hernandez, New Mexico*, 1941
- *Moon and Half Dome, Yosemite National Park*, 1960
- *El Capitan, Winter Sunrise*, 1968

Related books

Ansel Adams, *Examples: the Making of 40 Photographs*, Little, Brown, 1989

Ansel Adams: An Autobiography, Little, Brown, 1995

Website

www.anseladams.com

Cecil Beaton

Iconic celebrity photographs

- British royalty
- Film stars: Marilyn Monroe, Elizabeth Taylor, Grace Kelly, Greta Garbo, Marlene Dietrich

Related book

Cecil Beaton: Theatre of War, Jonathan Cape, 2012

Website

www.npg.org.uk (add search term *Cecil Beaton*)

Robert Doisneau

Iconic photographs

- *Les Pains de Picasso*, 1952
- *Musician in the Rain*, 1957
- *Pipi Pigeon*, 1964

Related book

Jean-Claude Gautrand, *Robert Doisneau 1912–1994,* Taschen, 2003

Website

www.robert-doisneau.com/en/

Elliott Erwitt

Iconic photographs

- *Segregated Water Fountains*, 1950
- *Mother and Child*, 1953 (Erwitt's wife and baby)
- *Dog Jumping*, 1989

Related books

Peter Mayle, *Elliott Erwitt's Dogs,* Te Neues, 2008

Eliott Erwitt, *Personal Best,* Te Neues, 2010

Website

www.elliotterwitt.com

Georg Gerster

Iconic aerial photographs

- *Labbezanga, Mali*, 1972
- *Grand Prismatic Spring, Yellowstone*, 1982

Related books

Georg Gerster, *The Past from Above: Aerial Photographs of Archaeological Sites,* J. Paul Getty Trust, 2005

Georg Gerster, *Paradise Lost: Persia from Above,* Phaidon, 2009

Website

www.georggerster.com

Andreas Gurksy

Iconic contemporary photographs

- *Paris, Montparnasse*, 1993
- *Chicago Board of Trade*, 1997
- *Nha Trang, Vietnam*, 2004

Related book

Andreas Gursky: Works 80–08, Hatje Cantz (bilingual editions), 2011

David Hockney

Iconic 'joiner' photographs

- *My Mother, Bolton Abbey*, 1982
- *Grand Canyon with Ledge, Arizona*, 1982
- *Place Furstenberg, Paris*, 1985

Related book

David Hockney, *That's the Way I See It*, Thames and Hudson, 2005

Website

www.hockneypictures.com

Alberto Korda

Iconic Cuban photographs

- *Don Quixote of the Lamp Post*, 1959
- *Rebels Riding into Havana*, 1959
- *Fidel Castro and Ernest Hemingway*, 1960

Related book

Alberto Korda, *Cuba by Korda*, Ocean Press, 2006

Website

www.havana-cultura.com

(add search term *Alberto Korda*)

Steve McCurry

Iconic photographs

- *Stilt Fishermen*, 1993
- *The World in Your Cup*, 2011
- *It Takes Two*, 2012
- *To Be Human*, 2012

Related book

Steve McCurry, *Portraits*, Phaidon, 1999

Website

www.stevemccurry.com

Martin Parr

Iconic tourist photographs

- *New Brighton*, 1986
- *Acapulco*, 2008

Related books

Martin Parr, *Small World*, Dewi Lewis, 2007

Sandra S. Phillips, *Martin Parr*, Phaidon, 2007

Website

www.martinparr.com

Sebastião Salgado

Iconic photographs

- Workers
- Migrants

Related books

Eduardo Galeano and Fred Ritchin, *An Uncertain Grace*, Thames and Hudson, 2004

Sebastião Salgado, *Workers: Archaeology of the Industrial World*, Phaidon, 1998

Website

www.amazonasimages.com

Thomas Struth

Iconic photographs

- Museum visitors
- Families

Related books

Dieter Schwarz, *Thomas Struth – Dandelion Room*, Artdata, 2001

T Bezzola, J Lingwood and A Kruzynski, *Thomas Struth: Photographs 1978–2010*, Monacelli Press, 2010

Website

www.thomasstruth32.com

Index